SAFE AT
SCHOOL

PowerKiDS
press
New York

WILLIAM DECKER

Published in 2017 by The Rosen Publishing Group, Inc.
29 East 21st Street, New York, NY 10010

First Edition

Editor: Theresa Morlock
Book Design: Reann Nye

Photo Credits: Cover (background), pp. 6, 24 (school) wavebreakmedia/Shutterstock.com; cover (child) rSnapshotPhotos/Shutterstock.com; p. 5 LuckyImages/Shutterstock.com; p. 9 SolStock/E+/Getty Images; pp. 10, 14, 24 (teacher) Monkey Business Images/Shutterstock.com; p. 13 Photographee.eu/Shutterstock.com; p. 17 iofoto/Shutterstock.com; pp. 18, 24 (friends) Sergey Novikov/Shutterstock.com; p. 21 Syda Productions/Shutterstock.com; p. 22 Nick Clements/DigitalVision/Getty Images.

Cataloging-in-Publication Data

Names: Decker, William.
Title: Safe at school / William Decker.
Description: New York : PowerKids Press, 2017. | Series: Safety smarts | Includes index.
Identifiers: ISBN 9781499427646 (pbk.) | ISBN 9781499429381 (library bound) | ISBN 9781499428636 (6 pack)
Subjects: LCSH: Schools–Safety measures–Juvenile literature. | Safety education–Juvenile literature.
Classification: LCC LB2864.5 D43 2017 | DDC 363.11'9371–d23

Manufactured in the United States of America

CPSIA Compliance Information: Batch #BW17PK: For Further Information contact Rosen Publishing, New York, New York at 1-800-237-9932

CONTENTS

We love **school**!

5

6

Our school is a safe place.

We walk in the halls.

We wait our turn.

We clean up our messes.

13

We are kind to **teachers**.

We tell a teacher when something is wrong.

We are kind to **kids**.

Fighting is wrong.

22

How do you stay safe
at school?

WORDS TO KNOW

kids

school

teacher

INDEX

WEBSITES

Due to the changing nature of Internet links, PowerKids Press has developed an online list of websites related to the subject of this book. This site is updated regularly. Please use this link to access the list:
www.powerkidslinks.com/safe/schoo